What Will Your Legacy Be?

By
Lydia M. Douglas

P.O. Box 2535
Florissant, Mo 63033

Copyright ©2013 by Lydia M. Douglas

Cover Designed by Sheldon Mitchell of Majaluk

Manufactured in the United States of America

Library of Congress Control Number: 2013902885

ISBN: 9780983486091

For information regarding discounts for bulk purchases, please contact Prioritybooks Publications at 1-314-741-6789 or rosbeav03@yahoo.com. You can contact the author at ldoug48305@aol.com.

What Will Your Legacy Be?

By
Lydia M. Douglas

PriorityBooks Publications
Florissant, Missouri

Table of Contents

My Favorite Quotes

Dedication

I dedicate the words of this book to every reader that has a heart to help others. Within the pages of this book I also want to pose an important question that will encourage each of us to examine or change our lives forever. Not just our lives, but also the lives of our children, family and others we come in contact with.

I also dedicate this book to my sons, Gerry, Mark and James, and hope their lives will touch their children and their neighbor's children.

I thank my beloved pastor, Dr. F. James Clark, Founder of Shalom Church City of Peace. I thank you for teaching and preaching the Word of God. In his teaching, I have learned that we all have a mission from God to do what He has told us to do.

We know Jesus is our role model, so on the Word of God we have to do as He did, reach out and love one another.

We are building our legacy by sowing one seed at a time. God wants us to have His comfort and to walk in His joy and peace.

As stated in 2 Peter1:2 "Grace and peace be multiplied unto you through the knowledge of God, and of Jesus our Lord."

Introduction

Webster defines legacy as: "something that has been passed on from an ancestor or predecessor."

What will your Legacy be? Is a thought that has been placed within my heart for a good reason? As I think about this topic and complete research for Legacy, I can focus on what it is I am doing to leave a memory on the hearts and minds of others.

This is a very strong question to think about. It helps to put our minds on things we need to think about as we consider, "What will my legacy be?"

I want to leave a strong mark on the heart of others. I want to know that my life will go on and on and that I will leave information or a legacy that I cared about others and wanted the best out of them. I want people to remember me, just as I have remembered those before me who have made an impression on my life.

As we considered what we can do to leave a legacy we must understand that we cannot go back and change yesterday, but we can begin to change our tomorrow and today. What a joy to know it is not too late to change!

Just a thought to think on!

What did you do today to help someone?

How do you want your life to be viewed now and in the future, and even when that unexpected day of death in your life comes?

Even though He is our Alpha and Omega, He does not tell us what or when the end will be. He just said do good to others and love your neighbors and your enemies as yourself.

I want my life to speak for me when that day comes.

What will your legacy be?

Chapter I

Legacy, defined by Webster's dictionary-"Something handed down from someone or an impression that is left on someone."

Something to think about: what will your legacy be?

Have you treated others the way you want to be treated?

Have your actions touched anyone in a positive way?

Each and every day we should focus on doing something that will leave a lasting affect or influence change in someone's life. If we reach only one person, then our work and living will not be in vain.

There is a Mahalia Jackson song that goes: "If I can help somebody as I pass along, then my living will not be in vain." This was the attitude my older family members had and they taught the same to me along the way. Their legacy has influenced my life for years.

So their living has been and is a legacy in my life. It's truly a rewarding feeling on the inside when you reach out and help others.

Let's live a life that someone will remember something we did or said that will have a lasting effect on his or her life.

Let's try our best to be the light that sits on a hill because we do not know who is watching or listening to us. We shall not light our candle and put it under a bush, we should want to reach out and help others. Sometimes it can be just a small thing that will be imparted into their lives forever.

We want to leave a smile on someone's face or some joy in his or her heart.

Are we living according to the morals and values that we were taught by our parents or elders that have touched our lives? If we are not, what can we do to get started?

NOTES

1 John 3:18 - My little children, let us not love in word, neither in tongue; but in deed and in truth.

Who do you admire? _____

_____
_____
_____
_____
_____
_____
_____
_____
_____
_____

What example of living have they left you to model? _____

_____
_____
_____
_____
_____
_____
_____
_____
_____
_____

Who encouraged you in your life? _____

_____
_____
_____
_____

What did they do to impress you? _____

Think about it!

Each of us has the capacity to be anything in this world today. There aren't any excuses that are big enough to stop you, at least there shouldn't be. Dr. Martin Luther King Jr. also did an awesome thing for the people of today. He has left a legacy that is still being taught and talked about today. If our ancestors did not fight to overcome, where would we be? Harriet Tubman led slaves safely to freedom in the Underground Railroad. If she didn't do that, imagine how life would be for the slaves of those days. That's her legacy?

Chapter 2

Things I was taught

I find myself repeating phrases that my mother and grandmother said. Some of the things I did not understand at the time, but as I get older they are becoming clearer and more understandable. Those are things that have been left upon me for a lifetime.

Just a few things that were taught to me:

Respect older men and women

Say yes ma'am and yes sir

Do as your parents say

Accept Christ in your life and you will be on the road of greatness

Always help others when you can

Do not do anything for others that you will not do for yourself

Always take care of your family

Love your husband or wife

Always say thank you

These are some wonderful things to teach your children as they are growing up. All kids need to understand what is expected of them, so it's important to teach them how to respect others and how to act. Each and every one of us should be taught how to love and give love. There is nothing greater than helping others and we do this because it is the right thing to do, but we also do it because we love people and were taught how to show that love.

When you teach your child about God and His love, it's hard not to understand what love means. We have to have the spirit to love unselfishly, and in doing so, we treat others with respect and kindness. That was my legacy from my parents and other elders who crossed my path in life. I've learned a lot and I want my legacy to be one of giving little nuggets of information that will inspire people to help others.

NOTES

Matthew 25:20 - And so he that had received five talents came and brought other five talents, saying, Lord, thou deliveredst unto me five talents: behold, I have gained beside them five talents more.

What did your elders teach you? _____

_____
_____
_____
_____
_____
_____
_____
_____
_____
_____
_____

Do you recall any nuggets or lessons that you live by now? _

_____
_____
_____
_____
_____
_____
_____
_____
_____
_____
_____

What is the most important thing you were told that encourages you to help others? _____

_____

Think about it!

Jesus told us to help the poor and defenseless. In Psalms 82:3, it reads, "Defend the poor and fatherless: do justice to the afflicted and needy." How do you respond to this? Are you doing what God asks of us? Are you leaving a legacy to help those in need?

Chapter 3

What Can I Do?

Now we can start thinking on what is it that we're doing or what can you do in order to leave a legacy for others.

How blessed we are when we sow good seeds in the path of others along the way. Looking beyond ourselves and looking toward others is pleasing to God.

We are building our legacy with every good deed we do and every good deed we do in the lives, heart and eyesight of others.

Let's think for a minute, "What type of impression am I leaving, or have I touched anyone's life in any way?"

What do you want said about you when that inevitable day we'll all face comes when you leave this earth?

No matter what trials or tribulations we go through, God said, "The battle is not yours, it's the Lord's."

Let's live a life that is pleasing in the eyes of God. No matter what we go through, treat it as a testimony that has been placed within us to share with others.

Our words might be the words someone might need to hear, that will and can leave a legacy on someone's life by one good deed at a time.

Sometimes a kind word will make a person's day. It could be family, friend, co-worker, or just a stranger. A good word will last a lifetime in the hearts and minds of others.

What will your legacy be?

NOTES

1 Timothy 6:18 That they do good, that they be rich in good works, ready to distribute, willing to communicate.

What are you doing that will sow good seeds? _____

_____

_____

_____

_____

_____

_____

_____

_____

_____

_____

Are you doing something in your life you want your family members to continue doing after you are gone from your earthly body? _____

_____

_____

_____

_____

_____

_____

_____

_____

What important message would you like to convey to others about your life? _____

_____

_____

Think about it!

For every good deed done, if the receiver pays that good deed forward by doing something positive for another person, what a wonderful world this would be. Be good to one another and spread happiness.

Chapter 4

Speaking in the Lives of Others

Now that we have time to think on what and how our legacy will be, let's think on maybe going in another direction.

How blessed will you be when you sow good seeds along the way? Looking beyond yourself, and looking toward others.

You are sowing good seeds with every good deed you do and every good seed you plant in the heart or eyesight of others. The Word of God states "His Word will not go out and return void."

Let's think for a minute, "What type of impression am I leaving or have I touched anyone's life in anyway?"

Proverbs 18:21: KJV

"Death and life are in the power of the tongue; and they that love it shall eat the fruit thereof."

Every word we speak matters. Something you say may seem insignificant to you, but to someone else those words can be life changing. When we speak goodness in the life of others we are depositing seeds that will last throughout eternity.

We as parents, grandparents, aunts, uncles, or friends, the young people need to be taught morals and values that will be a part of their lives now and in the future. The right word will and can take root and affect them many years to come.

All of the seeds of greatness that were implanted in my life have not left me.

Can we share those seeds with others? We all have seeds of greatness inside of us to be shared with others.

NOTES

Psalms 119:103 How sweet are thy words unto my taste! yea, sweeter than honey to my mouth!

Can you think of one good deed you've done? _____

_____

_____

_____

_____

_____

_____

_____

_____

_____

Think of a value you've learned from your parents. How could you use this to help others and leave a legacy? _____

_____

_____

_____

_____

_____

_____

_____

_____

_____

What kind of seeds could you plant in people to remember you by? _____

_____

_____

_____

Think about it!

If you help one person each day, how wonderful would you feel?

Chapter 5

That Great Day

What do you want said about you when that great day comes? And it will come. My husband passed away at the age of sixty years old.

A lot of good things were said about him, he truly left some good memories in the life of others.

With the good seeds that has been planted within us by family members, friends or even by strangers are to be shared with others. We are the fragrance of God to and for the next generation.

After all, we are building a legacy one good deed at a time. Sometimes a kind word will make a person's day. Good morning or good evening, you are looking good, etc. That just might be the one thing that will make a person's day.

I went to a home going service for a family member and his life truly did speak for the life he lived in such an awesome way. So many wonderful things were said about him, it really left a thought on my mind and I asked myself the question: "what will my legacy be?" You might not even know the person you are speaking about, but they will always remember what you did or said. You should have a plan for your life and when that great day comes, your life will speak for itself.

As we grow older physically and spiritually we should have a different perspective on life. It is not all about us; it is about living the life that God has allowed us to have.

Is that something to think about or what?

NOTES

John 15:9 - As the Father hath loved me, so have I loved you: continue ye in my love.

What will others say about you? _____
_____
_____
_____
_____
_____
_____
_____
_____
_____
_____

Do you think people will remember the good things you've done? _____
_____
_____
_____
_____
_____
_____
_____
_____
_____

How can you make sure your legacy is what you want it to be? _____
_____
_____
_____

Think about it!

There was a man who died and as the preacher gave the eulogy, he could not think of much to say about him. So he preached about everybody else getting saved. He said it's too late for this young man, but not for you. The only thing he really said about the person who had died was, "he died too young." He left a legacy that entailed criminal records, mischief and leaving his parents in pain. Is that a good legacy to leave behind? NO!

Chapter 6

What have I done today?

It does not cost anything to say hi or just to say a little joke or something funny to bring a smile or laughter to someone's life.

I go to my local gym and work out. I saw a tee shirt a young lady had on and it read, the best ribs and cake in town. I said something to her about it and we both had a good laugh. Hopefully she will remember how much we laughed about her shirt and it will bring a smile to her when she doesn't feel so happy.

The Word of God tells us in 1 John 4:11 KJV: "Beloved, if God so loved us, we ought also to love one another." Just being kind and nice to others, is showing love, and love is something you will not forget. When you show people love, it is wonderful to be remembered for it. Also, it is a way to build a legacy with every large or small deed done for others.

When we show love and kindness to others, we are in the plan of God.

1 John 2:10 KJV says: "He that loveth his brother abideth in the light, and there is none occasion of stumbling in him." When we do anything for others out of the kindness of our hearts that is showing the love of God. We are abiding in the light of God and there is no occasion where we will stumble as long as what we do is from our heart. That is building our legacy one act at a time.

For instance, I work with a group that sends packages to our soldiers overseas. We have adopted active soldiers in the United States Military and we send gifts at no charge to them or to their families. It is our hope that this act of kindness will continue as others join or start their own acts of kindness to show our soldiers how much we care and appreciate them. Also, the legacy will continue to live in the hearts of others who know about this activity as well as those who are recipients of these acts of kindness, whether we know them or not. God will be and is pleased with people when we act according to His will. God judges all of our hearts.

When we plant a good seed in the heart of others, they will not forget it.

We are to love others more that we love ourselves. The Word encourages us that "in lowliness of mind let each esteem others better than themselves." -Philippians 2:3b KJV.

Always ask yourself, "What will my legacy be?"

Remember, your legacy must have a beginning in order to have an ending. We want our ending to be better than our beginning.

There are many things you can do to begin to start your legacy. These are things your children or other people in your life can continue to carry on for you, after you are no longer able to, or when you die.

You can:

Help at the food pantry

Help the needy

Help your neighbor (everyone is our neighbor)

Visit the sick and shut in

Help out at the schools

At the end of each day, we should ask ourselves a personal

question.

Did I do anything to help someone today?

That is a very personal question that is between you and God, and Him alone whether you did or not.

NOTES

Proverbs 19:22 The desire of a man is his kindness: and a poor man is better than a liar.

How do you help others? _____
_____
_____
_____
_____
_____
_____
_____
_____
_____
_____

Have you worked in a food pantry, served the poor or volunteered for an organization? Why or Why not? _____
_____
_____
_____
_____
_____
_____
_____
_____
_____
_____

What can you plan to do to help others? Is this something you can get other family members involved in so it can continue into the future? _____
_____

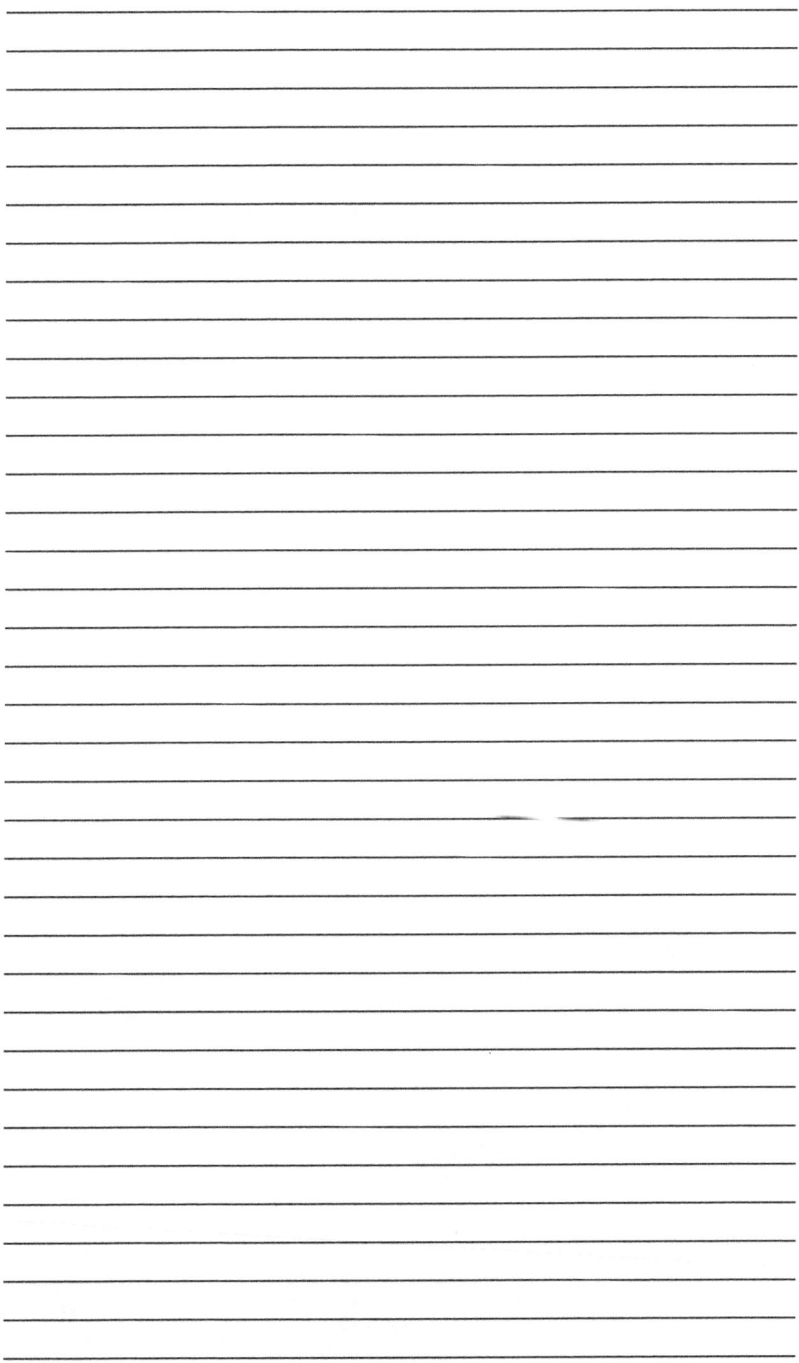

Think about it!

There are many families who spend holidays serving the poor and the hungry. Rather than them spending their money buying things they do not need, they donate to those in need. Helping others is a command from God. What is a legacy you and your family would like to do to help others?

Chapter 7

What Steps Are You Taking?

"The steps of a good man are ordered by the Lord." Psalm 37:23a KJV

If the Lord puts you in the path of someone or put someone in your path, do not hesitate to reach out and help in whatever way you can.

Remember, you are building your legacy and when you die, your life will speak for itself. Most of all, God will be pleased, that is our priority.

This is another day that we can ask ourselves a valuable question:

What did I do today?

Well first of all I did this today:

There was an older lady in the store shopping and she dropped a sweater and I picked it up for her. She said "Thank you very much." Of course I said, "You are very welcome."

I held a door opened for a lady

I allowed a lady to check out before me

I called and checked on my neighbor

I called several church members

I checked on my mother

You will have a very good feeling within your heart when you do a kind deed for others and you know that is pleasing to

God.

Isaiah 30:21 KJV

"And thine ears shall hear a word behind thee, saying. This is the way, walk ye in it, when you turn to the right and when you turn to the left."

This is a comforting Word from the Lord. When we are obedient to what He tells us to do, He is very pleased with our reaction to His command.

One day I was in the gym and I saw some money fall from a person's pocket. I went over to him and said, "I saw some money fall from your pocket." He was over joyed and happy. Now I could have waited until he left and picked it up and kept it for myself. I told him, "God's hand of wrath is much more than money." He said, "I agree, I would have done the same thing."

Now by my actions in this situation, I think, or I know, God is pleased with my decision. I know the man appreciated it. No one wants to lose their money.

That was just one thing I did on that day. Did I plant a seed in the person's life, well that is up to God; I just did what God put in my heart to do.

I want to leave some good thoughts in the minds of others. We do not cherish the praises of men, but of God. With each new day we have another chance to do something. It allows each of us to evaluate our daily living and to ask ourselves the question at the end of the day, "Did I do or say anything today that will help someone along the way that they will remember and hopefully will help them?"

NOTES

Proverbs 12:25 KJV "Heaviness in the heart of man maketh it stoop, but a good word maketh it glad."

Think of something you did to help someone. Was it hard to do? Did it take a lot of time? How did you feel after you did it?

_____

_____

_____

_____

_____

_____

_____

_____

_____

_____

How do you think others would feel if you helped them without them asking you to?_____ _____

_____

_____

_____

_____

_____

_____

_____

_____

_____

How often would you be willing to help others?_____

_____

_____

_____

Think about it!

It's a good feeling to help others. You don't walk away pulling your blouse or shirt away from your chest like look at what I did. But you feel good inside because you did an act of kindness. You have done the very thing that God expects us to do. You feel so good. So how do you think the receiver feels? They feel just as good! Do something kind for others because it is the right thing to do.

Chapter 8

What We Can Expect

In our daily walk we expect God to bless us, and on that same note we should be ready to bless others in whatever way we can. When we open our hands and share and help others, God will fill them once more.

After all, helping, loving, and caring for others are in the Will of God. We are to love others as we love ourselves.

"Cast not away therefore your confidence, which hath great recompense of reward. For ye have need of patience that after ye have done the will of God, ye might receive the promise." - Hebrews 10:35-36. KJV

All of the promises that God made to Abraham are ours as well if we walk by His command.

Our legacy is a conversation starter. Think about this. What do we have to share with others, as to what we have seen, done, or gone through?

To others, no matter if you are young or old, we should share our legacy. Someone, no matter their age, may need or may be looking for someone to help push them to get on the right path.

I have found nothing wrong with sharing my legacy with others. Our conversations should start and end with a powerful feeling with the ones you share it with.

NOTES

1 John 4:12 "No man hath seen God at any time. If we love one another, God dwelleth in us, and His love is perfected in us."

What is something you can do to show someone you love them? _____

_____

_____

_____

_____

_____

_____

_____

_____

_____

Do you have to buy something or make something?_____

_____

_____

_____

_____

_____

_____

_____

_____

_____

_____

How can you encourage others to show love to others through good works?_____

_____

_____

Think about it!

Visiting nursing homes and talking to the elderly is a good way to show your love. Many of them never receive visitors. This is a great way to do as Jesus ask us!

Chapter 9

Live the Life that we talk about

When we are thinking about building a legacy, we should include the young. When we consider what we can do with young people it should lead them into a leadership position.

Our lives and the positive things we are doing can be a changing agent in the lives others. What this means is when we show others something positive and worthwhile that we are doing to help others it will leave a positive impression on a young mind. Young people will hopefully turn around and emulate the same positive behavior.

When we help young people who are in need or who have not had anyone to show them any kindness, it changes how they see people. Too many people are afraid of teenagers, so they tend to ignore them or stay as far away as possible from them, keeping a safe distance. But these are the very people who need to be shown some kindness. How else will they learn to reciprocate?

What did I do today?

I gave a young man some money to buy himself some food to eat.

I held the door opened for two people and they said, "Thank you." I said, "You are welcome."

I waited and allowed a lady to open her car door and get in before I opened mine and she said, "Thank you." Of course I said, "You are very welcome."

My doctor's name is Dr. Fredrick Foster, a licensed Chiropractor who practices in St Louis, MO. I told him how much I appreciated what he has done and is doing for me. I have made some great changes in my life because of what he has done. When I am having a painful day, I remember what he told me and I do just what he instructed me to do and I feel much better. When ever I see him I always tell him, "I thank God for you." What he is doing in the lives of others is the gift God placed within his heart.

During our conversations he mentioned his family. That speaks volumes for the seeds they planted within him in the course of his youth and as a young man while growing up. Now many are reaping the harvest that has been planted within him. With everything he does for others, he is building his legacy, one patient at a time.

We all have two choices we can make that will be with us for many years to come. We can work and make a living for ourselves and we can design a life for ourselves and the ones that are coming behind us will have something to keep within their hearts forever.

That's another reason why we should put some thought into the life we are living in the presence of others and for ourselves as well.

I have learned that time is very important when measured up with our lives. We do not know when that time is up so let's do something that will speak for the life we have lived.

Time is our most valuable asset, yet we tend to waste it, kill it and spend it rather than invest it in the lives of others and that investment will be with them for a lifetime.

Life makes no guarantees as to what you will have and the type of life you will live. That is all up to you. It gives you the opportunity to make changes and choices.

Just as my grandparents and other older family members

that are gone on to a better place, but the things they taught me will be with me forever.

There is no reason to waste today; we are traveling through time into the future. Tomorrow is not promised to any of us. So on that note, let's try our best to leave a great legacy, not just a good one, a great one.

Is that not what we should do? After all, we might be planting the seed or watering it, but we know who is going to do the increase, God Almighty Himself.

My family planted some great seeds in my life. And they have not been in vain. All of this is building your legacy. You don't have to wonder what will be said about you when you die and people are discussing you. Most of all, God will be pleased and that is very important.

NOTES

John 13:34 - A new commandment I give unto you, that ye love one another; as I have loved you, that ye also love one another.

How can you be an example to others? _____

_____

_____

_____

_____

_____

_____

_____

_____

_____

_____

Do you think others would want to pattern their lives after you? Why or Why not?_____

_____

_____

_____

_____

_____

_____

_____

_____

What do you think others would say about you?_____

_____

_____

_____

Think about it!

Have you been a good steward for God? Have you set good examples for others to follow? How can you make sure your life is a good example for others? Most people want to leave a legacy of something positive to show they were here on earth and that they did something that mattered. Do you think this is true?

Chapter 10

Hospitality in Action

God has promised to reward us for doing what He has told us to do.

When I gave the young man money for food, the Word of God came to me and said, "I was hungered and ye gave Me meat, I was thirsty and ye gave me a drink, I was a stranger and ye took me in." Matthew 25:35 KJV

Yet, I was only doing something that was natural to me. I wasn't helping the young man to impress him or anyone. I did it because it was in my heart to do so.

My stepfather, which is the family member that I had mentioned earlier in the book, is the one I saw his legacy come to the forefront of my life. He took in family members at an early age and raised them, and the joy they shared about their life with him was just wonderful. His life was speaking for itself.

The word of God tells us that whatever we do to man, we are doing it unto the Lord, as illustrated in Matthew 25:40.

God will reward us for all of the good deeds we do. So whenever we have a chance to share or just do good for others, we will be rewarded for it.

Man cannot repay us for the deeds done to and for others, only God can do that.

Kindness accomplishes much more than we know. It really is a good feeling to do for others.

What did I do today?

I saw an article in the local newspaper about this young lady who won several awards by working at her school and one of the local libraries. She won several awards that will help her get into three different colleges. I met her and her family at a local restaurant and I gave her three books that will inspire her to continue on. She was so happy and elated, and of course, so was I.

I saw a young homeless lady and I saw where she could use some socks, so I bought her a package of socks. I could see the holes in the ones she had on. She was very pleased. That could have been me. I was grateful that I could help. What we do unto others, we do it unto God.

I mailed four books to a young lady who I was told about. She won three college scholarships and was accepted in her choice of college, but she is still in her senior year in high school. If those small donations of seeds will help her, then God will do the increase.

I made a business call which led into personal business. The young lady I was talking with in the Customer Service Department told me she was going through some rough times, but was so glad she received a call from me; now she knows she can get her life in order. Was I planting or watering, I do not know. I do what is placed within my heart, the increase belongs to God.

Even though we might not see the end or know the result, that is not what God told us to do; we are to just do it and wait. When we do our part it will come to past as to what He told us to do.

We are building our legacy with each and every good deed we do, as long as we do it in the name of our Lord and Savior Jesus Christ.

We should want our lives to speak for itself. Our lives will be relived over and over again through the lives of others.

One last question:

What will your legacy be?

Chapter 11

Measuring Up...The Good and the Bad

In measuring your good deeds against the bad, ask yourself this powerful question; let's not get sidetracked: What will my Legacy be?

This is another day that has been given to us to get it right.

My question is still the same; did I do anything today that will help others? Will your good outweigh the bad?

I was at the hospital today and there were six young ladies standing in the hallway talking. I stopped and asked if they were nurses. They said, "No, we are nursing students."

I said, "I am very proud of all of you," and encouraged them to be the best nurses they could possibly be. The Word of God tells us "we will reap what we sow;" so you should be the best you can be, because one day you might need a nurse and the good that you sow into the lives of others will be brought back to you.

The smile on all of their faces was such a joy to me. To see just a few words could bring joy to the faces of these future nurses was uplifting.

When we do good to others, God is pleased with us and our actions.

NOTES

Hebrews 13:16 - But to do good and to communicate forget not: for with such sacrifices God is well pleased.

What are you using your skills to do to help others? _____

_____

_____

_____

_____

_____

_____

_____

Do you feel good when you help others? Why?_____

_____

_____

_____

_____

_____

_____

How do you think people feel when you assist them in getting something completed?_____

_____

_____

_____

_____

_____

_____

_____

Think about it!

God wants us to set examples of helping others. When we do things God expects, He smiles. God gave us so many talents and if we use them for good, I believe they will multiply.

Chapter 12

Deeds in Action

Hebrews 13:5-6 - "Let your conversation be without covetousness; be content with such things as you have. For He Himself said "I will never leave you nor forsake you. Then we can boldly say "The Lord is my Helper, I will not fear what man will do unto me."

So on that Word, we do not have to fear doing good to and for others. God is with us because He said He would never leave us. And in Him, I will trust.

What did I do on today?

I went across the street and closed my neighbor's mailbox.

So it is not about us, it is about God and doing good. Then our good will out weight the bad.

Romans 8:6 - "For to be carnally minded is death; but to be spiritually minded is life and peace."

And you will have peace when you do what is right, and not looking for feedback from man, but of God.

My daily question for myself is, "what did I do today that God would be pleased with?"

I had a free coupon for a 32oz. drink from the service station.

What did I do with it? I gave it to a lady that was about to buy a soft drink, I had another one and this lady said she had small kids; I gave her the one for some free donuts.

I was in a fast food restaurant and this young man said he was hungry but did not have any money. I bought him some food and he sat down and was eating with joy on his face. Jesus said in Matthew 25:42, "I was hungry and you feed me not…" Whatever we do for mankind we do it unto the Lord. The joy of the Lord is truly my strength and you should strive to make it yours.

John 13:15 states:

"For I have given you an example, that you should do as I have done to you."

So now we know we have an example, and we must follow the example that has been set before us. He did not come to be served but to serve. We are building our legacy with one good deed after another.

So what will our legacy be?

Let's go and sow good seeds in the lives of others in the name of Jesus Christ our Lord. When we do it God's way, we will reap what we sow.

Always remember, we are building our legacy one good deed at a time.

NOTES

Psalms 41:1- Blessed is he that considereth the poor: the LORD will deliver him in time of trouble.

What kind of volunteering do you do to help others? Do you work in shelters, food pantries, or help people individually? _____

_____

_____

_____

_____

_____

_____

_____

_____

Do you expect God to reward you because you have followed His words to help the poor?_____

_____

_____

_____

_____

_____

_____

Who do you like helping the most, elderly, children, the hungry, or people who don't have skills?_____

_____

_____

_____

_____

_____

_____

Think about it!

We are to be examples of God. When we help others, we are really helping ourselves. We are working to see God and every time you do something good, you are making a difference. For every step you take to do good in the name of Jesus, you can expect, God to be pleased. Isn't that what most of us really want?

My Favorite Quotes

Quotes:

"I can't do everything, but I can do something to help someone, and what I can do, I will do." Oseola McCarty

"Special people in the eyes of God are the ones that have the ability to share their lives with others." Deanna Beisser

"There is no reason to waste today. You are traveling through time into the future. Tomorrow is beyond here and now." Deanna Beisser

I Peter 4:9-10

"Use hospitality one to another without grudging. As every man hath received the gift, even so minister one to another, as good stewards of the manifold grace of God." KJV

Ecclesiastes 9:10

"Whatsoever thy hands findeth to do, do it with thy might; for there is no work, nor device, nor knowledge, nor wisdom, in the grave, whither thou goest."

Deuteronomy 6:18A

"And thou shalt do that which is right and good in the sight of the Lord, that it may be well with thee."

Words to Remember Every Day

Be patient today with others,

They need someone who will take the time to listen

Be giving today with others,

They need someone who will share

Be honest today with others,

They need someone whom they can trust

Be sincere today with others,

They need someone who really cares

Be understanding today with others,

They need someone who is not judgmental

Be happy today with others,

They need someone who will smile

Life challenges us all each and every day,

That is why, it is important to remember....

Be gentle today with others, they need someone to be a friend.

-Anonymous

My Friday Story...Smile

A smile costs nothing, but gives much

It enriches those who receive, without making poorer those who give

It takes but a moment, but the memory of it sometimes lasts forever

None is so right or mighty, that he can get along without it

And none is so poor, but that he can be rich by it

A smile creates happiness in the home, fosters good within business, and is the countersign of friendship

It brings rest to the weary, cheer to the discouraged, sunshine to the sad,

And it is nature's best antidote for trouble

Yet it cannot be bought, begged, borrowed, or stolen, for it is something that is of no value to anyone, until it is given away

Some people are too tired to give you a smile

Give them one of yours, as one needs a smile so much as he who has no more to give.

So pass your smile on to others, and the Lord will Bless

There are no catches or rules

Just this simple test.

Anonymous

Tomorrow....Another Chance

If we might have a second chance

To live the days once more

And rectify mistakes we've made

To even up the score

If we might have a second chance

To use the knowledge gained

Perhaps we might become at least

As fine as God ordained

But though we can't

Retrace our steps

However stands the score

Tomorrow brings

Another chance

For us to try once more.

Happiness is found on the journey;

It's not the destination.....

So with each and every day we are given, that is another chance to do it God's way.

Anonymous

Did I

Did I help someone to realize a dream they thought they'd lost?

Did I listen when someone told me the reward is worth the cost?

Did I praise someone for their efforts and encourage someone toward their dreams?

Did I help someone to understand the end never justifies the means?

Did I make someone laugh and smile when they would much, rather frown?

Was I the one who picked them up when everyone put them down?

Am I, the one they confide in and know their conversation secure?

Did I provide them with someone to trust in knowing their friendship will always endure?

Am I humble and constantly striving to become more than I was yesterday?

Did I focus on the successes of others and follow through with all that I say?

If I constantly strive to become the one who can say I did to did I's.

Then my life is fulfilled, knowing I have achieved life's greatest prize.

Carl Morris

Footprints

When I felt lost and filled with pain,

Falling on my knees to pray, I had to explain.

How my heart ached, losing my soul mate,

I knew Lord You would help me, the pain to eliminate.

You picked me up when I was down,

And planted my feet back on solid ground.

I thank You Lord for blessing me,

Even though I lost someone special to me.

When I had no strength to carry on,

You took my hand like a newborn.

I made it through this heartbreak and pain,

I know whatever I go through,

You will be there again.

There was one footprint in the sand,

Because you picked me up,

and kept me close at hand.

I love you for carrying me through a lion's den.

For that I can say, Thank You God and Amen.

By RM Jackson

NOTES

Others Books by Lydia M. Douglas

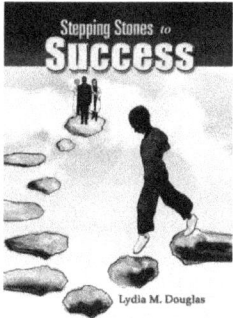

Stepping Stones to Success is a collection of essays that will reveal new paths and directions to motivate and inspire the readers to reach their highest goals.

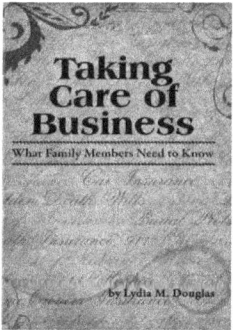

Taking Care of Business asks the question "Is your family prepared to handle your estate once you depart from this world." Have you mapped out your preferred funeral and burial plans?

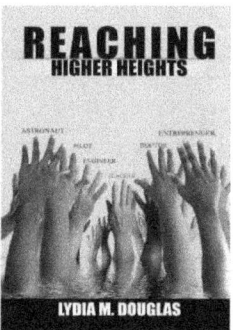

Reaching Higher Heights outlines effective strategies and goals to help students accomplish their dreams. Relevant to students of all ages!

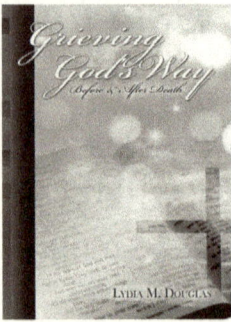

Grieving God's Way After thirty-nine years of marriage, Lydia M. Douglas' soul mate entered into eternal rest. Rather than succumb to bouts of depression and agonizing mental pain associated with the grieving process, Douglas accepted the comfort of her Heavenly Father. She chose to Grieve God's Way, the only way that would guarantee eventual peace and the stamina necessary to move on.

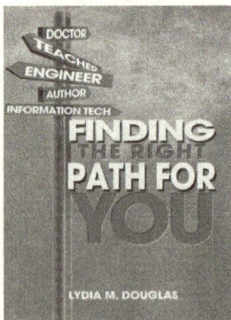

Finding the Righ Path for You Fear of the unknown is the main reason many teenagers fail to make informed decisions about their lives. What these teenagers don't realize is that the only wrong decision is making no decision.

To request information regarding presentations or to order books e-mail me at:
ldoug48305@aol.com
www.booksbylydia.com or
www.prioritybooks.com.
She is also available for student workshops.
Phone: 314-741-2532 or 314-608-9279